For Sister Mary _____,
May God liberate us
in His love.
Love,
Stephan Grosso

HARRY

My Friend

Stephan Grosso

LIGUORI
PUBLICATIONS

One Liguori Drive
Liguori, Missouri 63057
(314) 464-2500

The pictures of Harry Guttenplan on the front cover and inside this book are by Dr. Frederick Franck, whose drawings and paintings form part of the permanent collections of the Museum of Modern Art, the Fogg Museum, and the Tokyo National Museum. Commenting on Frederick Franck's renditions of Harry, Stephan Grosso wrote: ''These drawings by Dr. Franck are uncanny. He has seized the 'image and likeness of God' in Harry.''

Imprimi Potest:
John F. Dowd, C.SS.R.
Provincial, St. Louis Province
Redemptorist Fathers

Imprimatur:
+ Edward J. O'Donnell
Vicar General, Archdiocese of St. Louis

ISBN 0-89243-247-0
Library of Congress Catalog Card Number: 85-82391

"There was a rich man, who was clothed in purple and fine linen and who feasted sumptuously every day. And at his gate lay a poor man named Lazarus, full of sores, who desired to be fed with what fell from the rich man's table; moreover the dogs came and licked his sores. The poor man died and was carried by the angels to Abraham's bosom. The rich man also died and was buried; and in Hades, being in torment, he lifted up his eyes, and saw Abraham far off and Lazarus in his bosom. And he called out, 'Father Abraham, have mercy upon me, and send Lazarus to dip the end of his finger in water and cool my tongue; for I am in anguish in this flame.' But Abraham said, 'Son, remember that you in your lifetime received your good things, and Lazarus in like manner evil things; but now he is comforted here, and you are in anguish. And besides all this, between us and you a great chasm has been fixed, in order that those who would pass from here to you may not be able, and none may cross from there to us.' And he said, 'Then I beg you, father, to send him to my father's house, for I have five brothers, so that he may warn them, lest they also come into this place of torment.' But Abraham said, 'They have Moses and the prophets; let them hear them.' And he said, 'No, father Abraham; but if some one goes to them from the dead, they will repent.' He said to him, 'If they do not hear Moses and the prophets, neither will they be convinced if some one should rise from the dead.' ''

Luke 16:19-31

1

One February morning I stepped out of my Bronx apartment. Freezing winds pounced on me from deep blue skies. *Oh, what a beautiful day,* I thought, *but what a day to be out and to have no home.*

Indeed the six-block walk to the subway was frigid. I turned a corner and the winds knocked the breath out of me. From out of the skies, from off the tops and sides of buildings, the winds came. By the time I got to the subway I was numb with the cold.

Nevertheless, I decided I would get off at 86th Street and Lexington Avenue, one stop before 79th, so I could walk the five blocks to work. I did this sometimes. It meant putting off for ten minutes the unrelieved tedium of office work. I was like Sisyphus, who forever pushed uphill a heavy stone which always rolled down again. I rolled my stone every day when I went to work. Like Sisyphus, I liked taking advantage of the lull between the rollings of the stone — to meditate on life and people, to look up in wonder at the towering Manhattan buildings.

On this morning I came up the subway stairs from the south side of the corner; I usually came up from the north side. I pulled on my gloves, and braced myself for the winds I expected from all sides. As I reached street level I saw a strange-looking man. I had never seen him before. He stood on the sidewalk by the curbing, between two parked cars. A trash can stood on his right and a U.S. mailbox was on his left.

The man immediately struck me as someone existing outside of whatever was going on. People were going hither and thither, but he wasn't going anywhere. He stood on that street corner like a party of one — a lonely one facing the world. He seemed to be anchored to the spot as if he had always been there and would go on standing there long after the lights of the world went out, his chunky body leaning slightly forward, his left hand stretched out to the passing world. As I started to pass him, he opened his hand to me.

He reached out to me with such urgency that I stopped short, fished a coin out of my pocket, and gave it to him. He took the coin without looking at it, and in a thick, hoarse voice he said something. At first I thought he said "Thank you." He repeated it. I couldn't understand him — because I was eager to get away from him. I nodded my head in agreement and kept going. But as I passed down the street, his voice carried after me. There was a note in it that made me turn around and go back.

I stood before him and said, "What do you want?"

He tried to tell me. His face twisted, grimaced — strange gutteral sounds issued from his mouth. I shook my head. "I don't understand you," I said. He tried again. I was about to walk away when suddenly the sense of what he was trying to say leaped at me.

"Coca-Cola?" I asked. "Did you say Coca-Cola?"

"Yessir," he said clearly enough.

He wanted me to get him a container of Coca-Cola. I was so glad to understand the poor man that I didn't question his absurd request. He was, after all, asking to drink ice-cold soda in freezing February weather.

"Where shall I get it?" I asked. The man's eyes twinkled. With his left hand he pointed to a luncheonette a few doors up the street. "Okay," I said, "I'll be right back."

The counterman in the luncheonette seemed to know for whom I wanted the soda because he winked at me as he handed me the container of soda with crushed ice and a straw in it. Back to the corner I went. As the man saw me coming with the soda, he became excited. What he said sounded like, "Thanks champ, thanks champ!"

The moment I placed the straw under his mouth, the man began sucking up the soda with such vehemence that it ran down the sides of his mouth. Mucous also began oozing from his nose, down over his mustache.

I looked away. Indeed, I didn't know where to look; the man embarrassed me. It felt awkward standing there on the street in such cold weather, holding a container of ice-cold soda to this stranger's lips. I had the feeling that the whole world was looking at us.

As the man drank, the winds buffeted us with particular violence. I shivered. Even with my heavy winter coat I shivered. The man, however, wore only a navy jacket, and was hatless. How could he stand it? And how could anybody be so thirsty in such weather? I could see the man was handicapped, although I had not looked at him very closely. I saw that he had only one good hand; the other hand hung short and useless at chest level. I couldn't figure out what was the matter with it — except that the hand was grotesquely withered, the fingers twisted like a pretzel. Something was also the matter with his right leg because part of a crutch stood out from his left side. The partly concealed crutch made him look slightly tipped on the sidewalk. At the angle I saw him, he seemed to defy gravity.

But there we were, the pair of us — I holding the container of soda up to his mouth, hoping to high heaven he'd hurry so I could leave, the man sucking up the soda with a look of the frantic in his eyes. In the meantime the subway below us emitted the underground roars of arriving and departing trains. It kept discharging patrons who, on reaching street level, sped off in different directions. I didn't dare look around to see whether anybody was looking at us. I just counted the seconds until he would finish, so that I could leave. The February winds kept rushing every which way, crackling and booming like ocean surf. Down between the walls of tall buildings went the winds, swooping through the streets, veering into building fronts, shearing off into distant, uncanny whistlings. And here was this man, sucking up the last of the soda as if his life depended on it. His protruding eyes were fixed on the container — as if his gaze had the power to keep the container before him.

When at last he finished, I threw the empty container in the trash can nearby. I said, "Okay." In other words: "I did what you asked me, now let me go."

The man's eyes twinkled. Then, with his thick, gravelly voice he shouted after me — for I had turned away — ''God love you, God love you!'' I sped down the street. I turned to look back once. The man stood leaning on his crutch, with his head lowered like a buffalo, gazing after me with a look at once kindly and sly.

At the bottom of the street I turned the corner. I felt a strange tightening in my throat. Tears filled my eyes. I don't know why, but the stranger had moved me.

2

The next day I got off at the same subway station, 86th Street. It was 8:15 A.M. — as cold as the morning before. There the man stood, with his rather large head cocked to the side, leaning slightly forward on his crutch. As I came up from the subway, he seemed to be looking for me. He greeted me with a voice that sounded like a growl. "Hi champ, hi champ!" He promptly let me know what he wanted: Coca-Cola. I went to get it.

Back at his side, with container and straw placed to his mouth, I looked him over. He was probably of middle height, though he looked shorter. He was stocky, a bit stoutish around the middle, and he had thick gray-black hair. His bushy eyebrows went with the thick, coarse sideburns that ran down below his ears. His jaw was squarish and powerful, with a growth of grizzled hair on it. A thick handlebar mustache hung over his lip. He looked like an old-fashioned prizefighter, and his gravelly voice matched his appearance. His eyes, though, seemed to have nothing to do with the rest of him; they were remarkable eyes, slightly protruding, intensely blue. They were eyes one might see in some supremely gifted genius or holy man — a holy man who had passed through incredible stages of suffering, who had immersed himself in great life-changing experiences and had arrived at a childlike purity and simplicity.

"God love you, God love you," he said through strangled gasps and moans as he sucked up the soda with that same almost frantic look in his eyes. He lost hold of the tip of the straw. His mouth pursed to retrieve it, it eluded him, and he swallowed air. I put the straw to his mouth again. His coordination became confused; instead of sucking up the soda, he blew down through the straw and produced a gurgling, wheezing noise at the bottom of the container. The man kept blowing, determined to have his soda. At last he firmly got hold of the straw with his lip. He sucked on it with such violence that streams of mucous burst through his nostrils, trickling down over his mustachioed lip, some of it dripping off his chin. The cold February air soon froze it into greenish icicles.

I looked away. Again I had the feeling of inappropriateness, of awkwardness. At that moment I wished I had merely dropped a coin in the fellow's hand the day before and passed on. Why subject myself to this? After all, it was unpleasant to stand there in the bitter cold, trying to give soda to a man who couldn't even get it down his throat. On the other hand, it was not only the cold that bothered me. It was my standing there with a man whose plight was so public, whose suffering was so pitilessly visible. Surely people could see it. I looked again to see if anyone was watching us, or at least watching *him*. But no one was. Also, for some reason — I don't know why — I didn't want anyone to see that I was being kind to the man. I didn't want anyone to think I was feeling noble or good for stopping to give drink to a thirsty man. The truth is, I did not feel noble or good. The man's miserable condition distressed and humiliated me. It made me want to place myself as far away from him as possible.

Suddenly I noticed the man looking at me intently. I had been so preoccupied with my thoughts that I'd forgotten him. The way he studied me gave me the feeling that he might have discerned what I was thinking. Immediately I launched into polite phrases such as, ''There's no hurry — take your time. Enjoy it.'' I might have been kidding him, but I wasn't kidding myself. I had had enough of this bizarre man, balancing on his crutch, wearing summer-weight clothes, and guzzling ice-cold soda in February.

When he finished drinking, I dropped the empty container into the trash can and hurried down the windblown street without looking back.

3

For several days I skipped 86th Street and got off at 79th. *Really,* I told myself, *there's no reason why I should make it a habit. Surely someone is providing the man with ice-cold soda all this time. Someone must be getting it for him because the trash can nearby is filled with empty soda containers.*

Nevertheless, every morning when I passed the 86th Street subway station on my way to work, I remembered the man. I had an image of him leaning on a crutch with his hand outstretched. As if from another world, the hand reached out over an abyss. The man would flit out of my mind as easily as he flitted in. I moved easily into the press of my other problems and all the familiar realities of my life.

* * * *

I did not stop myself to ask why, but on the third morning — a Friday — I found myself getting off at 86th and Lexington. I was to return the next day, and the next. I simply got into the habit of getting him his soda, giving him a coin, and then going on to work. Nor did I let it bother me that mucous oozed out of the man's nose when he drank his soda. And too, it stopped mattering whether people stared at us or not. The soda I brought him provided the poor man with such satisfaction that it was worth the trouble.

One day I learned the man's name: Harry. That made it easier. Soon my visit with Harry at 8:15 in the morning became a sort of ritual. He greeted me with the words, "Hi champ, hi champ!" (I suspect he called everyone champ) the minute he saw me come up from the subway.

He said, "Get me a Coke?"

I said, "Sure."

After he had his Coke and the coin I gave him, we exchanged pleasantries for a minute. Everything Harry tried to say came tortured from his lips. He didn't stammer, he simply had a pronunciation problem; his vocal chords and brain simply refused to coordinate. He tended to slur over his words, mumbling them as if he were drunk. (I found out the cause of his problem much later. He had had a stroke.) After we chatted a bit we wished each other a good day, and I started down the street. Harry invariably shouted after me, "God love you, God love you!" He uttered these words with enormous energy and feeling — and he uttered them clearly. I turned, with a wave of my hand, and shouted back, "And God love you, Harry."

* * * *

One day I asked him where he lived.

"Bronx," he said.

"Well, can I visit you sometime, Harry?"

"Sure," he said. "Sure, champ."

That's how I happened to start visiting Harry every week, usually on a Thursday evening after work. He lived in a low-rent project in a two-room apartment paid by Welfare. His neighbors were black and Puerto Rican. The building had an elevator, an advantage to Harry with his crutch.

I remember the first time I visited Harry. The lobby was crowded with mothers and their children. The elevator came, and they all rushed in. When they saw that I was left standing outside the elevator, they all squeezed back inside to make room for me.

I got off at the fifth floor. Heavy cooking odors drifted through the long L-shaped corridor. Sounds of children, television, and radio came through the closed doors. I went looking for Harry's apartment number: 5-D. I went up and down the corridor several times; the lighting was poor. At last I found the door that had "D" on it and knocked loudly. No sound. I knocked again. This time I heard stirring from within.

"Is that you, champ? Is that you?"

"It's me, Harry," I answered.

A series of grunts and wheezes followed. "I'm coming, Steve," I heard him say in his gravelly voice. Another pause. Then I heard a curious rattling noise. From the sound, I gathered that Harry had gotten out of his chair and, inch by inch, was coming to the door. It sounded as if he was dragging something after him.

Two or three minutes passed before the door opened. I stepped in. The odor in the apartment was overpowering; it smelled of urine and decayed food.

"Hi champ, hi champ!" Harry said excitedly. He was standing there in his underwear with his socks and shoes on. As I passed around him to get from the vestibule to the kitchen, Harry turned around slowly on his crutch and followed after me. Now I understood why he moved with such difficulty; the strange rattling I had heard from outside the door was Harry's withered right leg. It was a skinny stick of a leg that trembled from the slightest exertion. He dragged it alongside his thick, normal-sized left leg.

I watched Harry's laborious stint from the door to his chair. Using his crutch, he inched along on his good leg until he reached the easy chair. Turning around slowly, he teetered for an instant on his one leg, then slumped back into the chair. I could not help noticing litters of crumbs and bits of food clinging to the arms of his chair and on the floor around his feet. Again, the stench from his unwashed body was overpowering.

Once Harry was seated I got up and looked around. His apartment had two small rooms. The furniture was ratty; it looked donated or picked up from the street. The bedroom had a queen-sized bed and an old dark-colored chest of drawers. A tiny night table stood by the bed with a gold-colored lamp on it. The other room was a combination living room and kitchenette. In it was the recliner chair that Harry sat on. Along the wall was a big, battered, green-colored sofa, and opposite the sofa was a small, old-fashioned dresser with a folding mirror. The kitchen had a table and two chairs. A lampstand stood on the left side of Harry's recliner. Squarely in the center of the room was a television set atop a wooden stand. The picture on the screen was flipping, and a babble of voices came out of the loudspeaker. That was it.

Having looked over his humble little apartment, I went back to the kitchen chair opposite Harry and sat down. I said, "You have a nice place, Harry."

Harry appeared to be studying me with his slightly protruding blue eyes. I had the feeling he was seeing me for the first time. Perhaps he was curious to see what sort of fellow he had invited now that I stood in the familiar surroundings of his own apartment. Perhaps I, too, wanted to see him away from the milieu of a street corner. And so we sat there, each looking the other over. As if to assure himself, he said, "Hi, champ." And I said, "Hi, Harry."

Harry sat in his chair like a man enthroned. He kept looking me over, but somehow I felt I had passed the first test. Again I said I thought he had a very nice apartment. Having said that, I did not know what else to say and Harry did not pick up on it. If he heard me, he gave no sign. He just sat and stared at me. I searched for something to say to break the uncomfortable silence.

At last I thought of something to ask him: What was his Christian denomination? Harry frequently uttered the words "God love you," and he had once asked me for a crucifix. I presumed he was Christian. I didn't think he was Catholic; I thought he was Lutheran, probably because the Yorkville part of Manhattan is German-American. So his reply took me by surprise.

"I'm Jewish, Steve," he said.

I found it hard to believe. Jewish? A Jewish beggar in New York?

I looked at him closely. Harry had the look of a German, a Prussian-German, at least according to my idea of what

Prussian-Germans are supposed to look like. That is, he had bushy eyebrows, bristly hair on his head, a grizzled mustache, a jutting jaw, and a barrel chest. If Harry had put on a German helmet, I would have mistaken him for the Kaiser. But how explain a New York Jew begging in the streets of Manhattan and uttering the words ''God love you'' to anyone who was the slightest bit kind to him? How explain his asking me for a crucifix when, for some Jews, the crucifix is simply a sign and memento of troubles? Also, in New York City — which has more Jewish social and philanthropic agencies than anywhere in the country — how could Harry have been bypassed? Had he no family? I tried to find out.

But getting information from Harry was very frustrating. He seemed willing to tell me anything I wanted to know, but it was hard for him to say it and equally hard for me to understand him. Harry was as frustrated as I was. Sometimes he would go into a tantrum. His face would redden, his eyes would pop with anger, and he would repeat the word or phrase over and over again. When the word or phrase that made everything clear finally got through to me, I would repeat it after him to show I understood. Then Harry would be relieved. His eyes would lose the shine of anger and take on a twinkle. I, too, would be relieved.

Harry spoke largely in monosyllables or in very short sentences. Sometimes I could understand him clearly. I thought at first that Harry was mentally deficient, but as I got to know him I changed my mind. He was not only intelligent, he was sensitive. And he was not only sensitive but, as I was to find out, profoundly generous, even though he was the poorest man I knew.

I began to think Harry might have a hidden life deep within himself, a life he could not put into words. Perhaps he had repressed himself for so long and gathered such a load of unexpressed feeling that he dared not try to drag it up out of himself. He had a habit of saying "I feel so alone" or "I am sad today" or "I'm very discouraged." These were feelings that hinted at what might have been going on in the man.

The best I could do was to hear Harry out when he had something to say. Often what he had to say did not come to very much, and saying it was such an enormous undertaking for him that I wondered if it was worth the trouble. Certainly for Harry it seemed worth it. I had the feeling that the act of communication was something sacred to Harry, like prayer. It was something he had to do; above all, he had to be understood.

I was to find out that Harry did have a family. I also learned that his impaired speech was due to two strokes he had had. He also suffered from asthma and a sort of chronic bronchitis that kept his throat and chest continually clogged with phlegm. To top it off, he had been struck with two terrible childhood diseases — polio and sleeping sickness.

4

One day I asked Harry if he had a favorite food. "Ham,"
he said. I asked him if there was anything else he liked. He
beamed the words out: "Potato salad."

So, the next time I came I brought him ham and potato
salad. I knocked on the door, expecting to hear Harry say, "Is
that you, Steve?" I knocked again and waited to hear him
struggle out of his chair. I visualized him maneuvering into
position, then slowly shuffling, as the floor creaked under
his weight and his bad foot dragged after him, until at last he
slowly swung the door open. But I waited in vain. Nothing
happened, although I heard a faint stirring from within. I
called out: "Harry, are you all right?"

Silence.

I called out again. "Harry, are you all right?"

Silence.

I knew Harry was at home. I shouted, "What's the matter, Harry?" Suddenly I heard his voice cry out, "Steve, Steve, Steve. . . . "

The words came through the door so breathlessly fast that I was alarmed. What could be happening to him? I shouted through the door, "I'll be right back, Harry — wait!" Then I went looking for the superintendent. The superintendent would have to open the door. Poor Harry, I thought; he might be mugged and lying on the floor in a pool of blood. Yet, at the same time I could not help wondering what in heaven's name anyone would mug him for. He was absolutely penniless!

The superintendent explained to me that it was unlawful for him to enter rooms occupied by tenants — only housing project police had the authority. Yes, I said, but wasn't this an emergency? The man was sick and might have been mugged. Couldn't he open the door? The man said he could not. Well, could he tell me where I could find the housing project police? The man shrugged, he had no idea.

I went searching for the housing project police who, in an area of several square blocks of houses, could have been anywhere.

Dusk was falling rapidly, piling up shadows in the corners. Groups of black and Puerto Rican children played in the great courtyards set between each house. A strange twilight world it was: trees, hedgerows, mini-parks, and children everywhere whooping and squealing at play. I crossed one street after another, carrying Harry's bag of ham and potato salad under my arm. I wondered whether I had passed the policemen without knowing it, since the waning evening light turned children and adults into silhouettes that I could barely distinguish. There was still a faint red glow in the sky where the sun had set — like a dash of red paint clinging to everything. After a bit the red melted into thin air, leaving the courtyards devoid of any real definition and wrapped in a gray, colorless half-light. The children played on, but now their shouts seemed to come out of nowhere and their movements in the half-light took on the appearance of indistinct pantomime.

By now I had covered the entire area looking for the security police, and I was on the verge of going to a nearby police precinct. But as I turned a corner there they were — the project police, standing casually near a building entrance.

A few minutes later we stood outside Harry's apartment. I knocked on the door, saying, "Harry, I'm coming in to see you." With that, the policemen opened the door and we trooped in.

Harry was seated with an apoplectic look on his face. He stared at me, then said, "Hi, Steve."

"What's the matter, Harry?" I asked.

Silence.

"What's the matter?"

He just stared at me with his large, blue, protruding eyes. His head was thrown slightly back, and his withered right hand was tucked under him like the fin of a seal.

"I guess he's all right," I said to the policemen. It was apparent that Harry hadn't been mugged or beaten. I thanked the men, and they left. Now that we were alone in the apartment, I reached for the ham and potato salad, hoping to cheer Harry with it.

"Look, Harry, I brought you your favorite dish." I uncovered the ham and the potato salad and placed it before him. "See?"

Harry continued to stare at me with that apoplectic look. I put the food in a dish, set it on a TV tray by his right hand. Harry immediately reached out and began eating. He ate in silence, tossing the food into his mouth with his good hand. I sat down in the kitchen chair opposite him, and wondered what to make of it.

After a while I said, "You gave me a scare, Harry. You sure did." Harry went on eating. "Harry, you have to give me a key, you know, so you don't have to get up when I come. Then I won't have to go chasing around if you can't open the door." Then I said, "Do you have an extra key, Harry?" Harry nodded. I settled back. "I'm glad you're all right, Harry." Harry stared at me. I kept talking. "Whew! What a long day. Couldn't wait to get off work. There was a train delay this morning — half an hour we waited. Drove me crazy. I . . . ."

Suddenly, right in the middle of my sentence, Harry raised his good hand and, as I stared in disbelief, started to thumb his nose at me. I can't say why this sudden, incongruous gesture brought hackles to my spine. But it did. It slightly terrified me. Harry sat there with his great blue eyes bulging out at me. He had his thumb pressed to his nose, with the fingers of his hand fluttering at me. While he was doing this, a mischievous smile slowly formed on his lips, giving him a look that was almost sinister. It was spooky.

The smile faded from his lips. The hand slowly descended and hung just above his knee. "Forgive me, Steve," he said. He tried to say something else, but I couldn't understand him. I felt amusement ripple through me at Harry's sudden reversal.

"Ah, Harry," I said, "there's nothing to forgive — is there?"

"I can't help it, Steve, I can't help it. Forgive me."

As he said these words his hand went up slowly, and I was again the object of Harry's nose and thumb. "I know you don't mean it, Harry," I said, laughing. As his hand went down, Harry repeated his regrets, apologizing profusely.

He repeated this several times more before I left him to go home. I tried to understand Harry's gesture, and I can only say that all of us have resentments, some of which are unconscious, which we conceal at times even from ourselves. Harry, of course, had good reason to feel resentful. But all I can do is speculate about what these resentments were and why he expressed them to me the way he did. Harry thumbed his nose at me other times I visited him, and I grew used to it — though, I must say, there was something spooky about it.

When I went to see him the following week, Harry explained that he had had a seizure just before I came to see him.

"I never know what I'm doing then, Steve," he explained, adding, "You're not mad at me?"

"Of course not, Harry," I assured him. "You couldn't help it."

5

Harry and I had a hard time communicating, although he didn't spare himself the effort when he had something to say. To tell me a simple thing like "I'm glad you came" required that he repeat himself a dozen times because I couldn't understand him. To spare him the violent effort that it took, I sometimes pretended to understand him. Harry wasn't fooled. He would look slyly at me and go on repeating the word or phrase until I understood him or until I distracted him from it.

Harry had a real need to disburden himself of things. That is why, when we got together, we spontaneously focused on him — on what he was feeling or what he wanted. He would tell me all kinds of things, no matter how unexciting or trivial. Harry had so little chance to have anybody listen to him. That is why, I think, there was something impenetrable about him. He had so much stored up inside himself that he had no room to take in what others had to say. Because he could not adequately say what was on his mind, he never quite caught up to himself. Most of the time he didn't even try; the struggle to be understood and the frustration that went with it made the effort too great.

As I became familiar with Harry's labored way of speaking, he began to tell me more about himself; and now and then he provided me with glimpses into his Jewish background. Just glimpses, but sometimes illuminating ones. Harry's blunt way of saying things in the fewest possible words revealed his family life in a way that a lot of words couldn't. He made me see how alike families are no matter what their culture or background.

This one evening, as we sat waiting for his TV dinner to heat, he suddenly said, "I'm very discouraged, Steve."

"What's the matter, Harry?"

"I don't know," he said, his eyes fixed on me. He blurted out, "I think I'm going to die, Steve."

I hastily contradicted him. "Oh, come on, Harry, don't talk that way — you're not going to die." My words sounded very inadequate. After all, how did I know? Harry continued to stare at me; he didn't seem very convinced. I jumped to my feet. "Come on, now — have something to eat. You'll feel better."

I put his TV dinner of spaghetti and meatballs before him, and put the fork in his hand. Harry lowered his eyes. He toyed with a meatball for a while before bringing it to his mouth. When the meatball finally did enter his mouth, it seemed to stick in his throat. I poured him a glass of soda, and said, "Drink some soda, Harry." Harry just sat on his throne-like recliner, fork in hand, staring thoughtfully ahead.

His disgruntled, unhappy look saddened me. I wondered whether Harry needed to be with people more than he was. Was it enough to see me once a week? Couldn't something more be done for him, something that his family had overlooked? It seemed to me that, although his physical handicaps were severe, what he must find hardest to bear was simple loneliness. I didn't think that my visiting him once a week provided enough human contact. He needed much more. So when I went home that night, I wrote a letter and sent it to several social work agencies. It read:

Dear Sir,

I am writing with regard to my friend, Mr. Harry Guttenplan, aged sixty-one years old. He is in need of help. In childhood he contracted "sleeping sickness"; a year later infantile paralysis. These diseases have left him permanently crippled (both his right arm and leg failed to develop in proportion to the rest of him). Mr. Guttenplan barely gets around on a crutch. He is very poor (no income although Welfare pays his rent), and he lives by himself. He finds the latter hardest of all. I am sure you will understand the loneliness and isolation of this man. He lives in two small rooms; his movements in such close quarters are highly restricted — from bed to chair and from chair to bed. Although his sister and her husband visit him daily to feed him and put him to bed, and I visit him once a week, it just isn't enough; he needs more human contact. The last time I saw Mr. Guttenplan he complained of feeling "disgusted," adding that he didn't expect to live much longer. Not very happy thoughts.

I have heard that your service agency operates a home-bound unit for handicapped persons, for those who are unable to travel on a bus or subway. If so, can't Mr. Guttenplan be taken to your rehabilitation center on a once-a-week basis, and there have the chance to meet people, if possible people of his own age? He can be encouraged to take part in social things. Later he might be given some kind of vocational training — anything to get him to hope again. Mr. Guttenplan's use of his left hand is good; his muscular control is slow but accurate. He is intelligent, though handicapped with a speech problem. He has difficulty pronouncing words clearly.

Please let me know whether your agency can help him. I will withhold Mr. Guttenplan's address (he lives in the South Bronx, near East 138th Street) until I hear from you.

I thought it best to omit certain things in the letter lest I prejudice the agency and it refuse to help Harry. I couldn't say that Harry's brother-in-law drove him every morning to the corner of 86th Street and left him there for four hours to beg on the street. The idea might not appeal to the agency. I also thought it wise to leave out the fact that Harry had had two strokes. I sent the letter, and received several responses. Jewish Family Services sent a young social worker. I did not expect this to distress Harry, but it did. Harry had a fit.

I hadn't connected Harry's uncoordinated movements and occasional sluggishness with brain damage. The social worker took one look at Harry and said, "He's got brain damage."

He asked Harry a few questions. Harry stared apoplectically at the social worker. Then Harry turned to me and gave me a look which seemed to say, "What are you doing to me?"

I tried to tell him with my eyes that I was only trying to help him. I don't think he understood.

"You seem to be the creative one," the young social worker said, turning to me. "Does he make an effort to respond to you?"

I said I didn't know what he meant. Would he explain?

"I mean," he said, "does he try to meet you halfway? Does he cooperate? Is he doing anything to help himself?"

Harry was more alert and responsive than he appeared to be. I disliked talking about him as if he weren't there. "Harry's not feeling well just now, but he has much better days," I said. I winked at Harry. Harry only stared at me.

The social worker prodded Harry with a few more questions. Harry mumbled his replies. The social worker turned to me. "What is he saying?" I translated as best I could. The man got to his feet. "Well," he said, "there's not much we can do." He stayed a few minutes more and asked several questions. Then he left.

The social worker's visit left Harry an emotional ruin. Gone were his smiles and lighthearted mood. He sat in a daze. When I tried to ask him how things were, he turned and wouldn't speak to me.

6

Harry was still angry at me when I came the following week, and he showed it by not looking at me. I tried to find out what was the matter.

"You didn't like having the social worker come to see you, did you, Harry?"

"No, Steve."

"Why? He wanted to help you."

Harry didn't answer. He looked the other way.

"Don't you want to meet people, Harry?" Harry kept his face turned from me. "Are you mad at me?"

"Nope," he lied.

* * * *

One evening as I was visiting with Harry, the door opened and in walked a man.

"Hello, Harry," said the man. He turned to me. "Are you Steve?"

"Yes," I said.

"I'm Jack," the man said.

Harry said, looking at me, "That's my brother-in-law."

I said, "Nice meeting you."

The man was of middle height, about the same age as Harry, and powerfully built. (Harry told me later that his brother-in-law had been a prizefighter.) Jack had a rough way about him. Like Harry, he had difficulty speaking and being understood; his words slurred over one another. The two men barely acknowledged one another.

"I came to put him to sleep," Jack said.

"Steve's here — Steve can do that," rasped Harry.

The man didn't argue. "Okay," he said, and was gone.

There were other times when Jack walked in. He never stayed long. Sometimes he greeted Harry with the words, "Hello, ya bum." Harry would respond by scowling. The two men appeared not to like each other.

Yet, Jack, for all his rough ways, faithfully came by every morning and took Harry to the corner of 86th Street and Lexington Avenue. He left him there, as Harry himself put it, to "work." At about twelve noon Jack picked Harry up and drove him to his Bronx apartment. Harry's sister, Sylvia, now took over. She shaved him, washed him, and fed him. In the evening Jack came by again, on his way home. He would help Harry to his feet (rather roughly, I thought; I saw him do it once) and lead him to bed. Then he would leave. In the morning Jack would come by at 7:30, and the whole process was repeated.

Jack didn't have to stop in on Thursday evenings because I was there. But most Thursdays he looked in anyway, in case I might not have come. Yet, Jack and Harry were hostile to each other.

One evening I walked in and found Harry on the floor. I don't know how I managed to do it — he weighed over 200 pounds — but I lifted him to his feet and half-carried-half-dragged him across the room back into his armchair. Safe in his chair, he looked at me proudly.

"You're a true friend, Steve," he said.

He tried to explain what had happened. From what I gathered, he had slipped and fallen on his way to the toilet. He couldn't get to his feet, so for hours he lay on the floor in a pool of his own urine.

After mopping up the hallway and putting Harry's TV dinner in the oven, I sat down, looked at Harry, and said, "Harry, what the hell more can happen to you? Damn it, you can᾿ ᾿ven go to the toilet without winding up a casualty." I ᾿ ᾿k my head. "I can't understand it."

I didn't tell Harry what I couldn't understand. Strangely, it was Harry who brought out what I was thinking but hadn't put into words.

He said, "Steve, do you know who did this to me?" He had a slight smile on his face with a suggestion of mischief in it.

"You mean having all those things the matter with you?"

"Yup."

I said, "Who?"

"God," he said. "God did this to me."

I looked at him. Harry sat in his chair with the same faint

smile on his lips. He seemed to have calculated what the effect of his words would have on me. He was scrutinizing me, waiting to see what I might say. Frankly, I did not know what to say.

I said, "Yes, Harry." And I kept silent.

But when I went home that night I thought about what Harry had said. That he could say "God did this to me" was amazing. I never dreamed that Harry could be conscious of God in that way. There was reproof in his words, but something else was implied, too. It seemed to me that only a man who has sent up waves of protest and known that he was heard — by God — could have uttered such words. It meant that Harry had a relationship with God.

I, too, had been thinking along these lines, trying to square God's goodness with human suffering. The plight of Harry, and of millions in the world like him, contradicted it. I puzzled over the mystery of God and human suffering. It tormented me.

But I said nothing of this to Harry. Would it have helped him? In speaking about his suffering, Harry revealed a lot about himself. Still, he was, and remains even to this day, a mystery to me. In a sense I liken him to the plight of Job:

For he crushes me with a tempest,
    and multiplies my wounds without cause;
he will not let me get my breath,
    but fills me with bitterness.
If it is a contest of strength, behold him!
    If it is a matter of justice, who can summon him?
Though I am innocent, my own mouth would condemn
    me;
    though I am blameless, he would prove me perverse.

I am blameless; I regard not myself;
   I loathe my life.
It is all one; therefore I say,
   he destroys both the blameless and the wicked.
When disaster brings sudden death,
   he mocks at the calamity of the innocent.
The earth is given into the hand of the wicked;
   he covers the faces of its judges —
   if it is not he, who then is it?

(Job 9:17-24)

But at least the story of Job has one consolation: he was prosperous before his troubles, and after his troubles God made him prosperous again. Indeed, God gave Job twice as much as he had had before. Harry, in contrast, was poor from the beginning, his sufferings were unremitting, and, rather than improve, things had worsened. He was to die penniless.

Some weeks later I brought a bad cold with my visit to Harry. I grumbled and complained between taking out my handkerchief and blowing my nose. Harry sat and watched me suffer. I gasped and caught my breath.

"Damn this cold," I complained. Again I blew my nose, moaning and cursing under my breath.

Suddenly Harry blurted out, "I'll take it on me, Steve, I'll take it on me."

"What?" I said, dumbfounded.

"I'll take it on me, Steve." He meant he would take my bad cold on himself, suffer it in place of me.

Apart from his idea of sacrifice, which in itself was extraordinary, there was something else suggested. Somewhere I had read about "victim souls," persons born to suffer. As I understood it, these are people who have accepted inordinate and unrelieved suffering as their purpose in life. (The motives cited are several: to suffer in atonement for the sins of others, to give glory to God, etc.) It is a repellent notion. Yet, there are persons who, for reasons that are beyond us, seem to have everything the matter with them. From the day they are born to the day they die, they experience affliction with scarcely any relief. For example, leaving out his mental and emotional afflictions, how could you begin to explain the sheer number of Harry's physical afflictions?

At age fourteen he contracted "sleeping sickness" and lay in a coma for months, hovering near death. He recovered.

The following year, at age fifteen, he contracted infantile paralysis. The disease withered his right arm and leg, handicapping him for life.

He had high blood pressure. This caused him to have two strokes which resulted in brain damage. (He was to have a third stroke while I knew him.)

He had asthma: his nose, throat, and chest were continually clogged with mucous. His asthmatic attacks brought him close to asphyxiation.

His teeth were eaten away to dark stumps, a condition which limited what he could eat.

And last of all, he contracted Parkinson's disease, which attacks the nerves. It also affected the liquid balance in his body and made him inordinately thirsty. (This probably explains why he would drink ice-cold Coca-Cola in freezing temperatures.)

"Never mind, Harry," I said, smiling. "I'll take care of my own cold — you've got enough to worry about."

But I worried about it. This wasn't the first time that human suffering, mine or someone else's, confounded and outraged me. If, according to Christian theology, Harry was a victim soul, and if God had chosen him to suffer in this life more than most other people, what was the reason for it? What had he done? And what good could pain and suffering in itself accomplish?

I found it easy to understand punishment for wrongdoing. Surely there is good reason for punishing persons who, without cause or provocation, bring about the pain and suffering of others. But for cases like Harry's, I have never quite found a satisfying rational explanation. And so, I have set the question aside, unanswered.

But from the spiritual point of view, in a way that transcends the limitations of my intellect, I have grasped the strange, almost incomprehensible world of love, the love of Jesus that was so great that he suffered an ignominious death for us. His final commandment, that we love one another even as he loved us, is perhaps the key to the mystery of suffering. And here I shall have to let the matter rest.

7

On this autumn evening I came in with Harry's favorite ham and potato salad. It put him in a good mood. He started humming and his blue eyes sparkled. Suddenly he broke out in song:

Shine on, shine on harvest moon
   up in the sky.
I ain't had no lovin' since January,
   February, June or July.
Snow time ain't no time to
   stay outdoors and spoon.
So shine on, shine on harvest moon
   for me and my gal.

Harry grinned. I applauded madly. "Hey, that's great, Harry — where'd you learn to sing?" Harry never heard me. He had resumed his singing:

Swanee, how I love you, how I love you,
    My dear old Swanee.
I'd give the world to be
    among the folks in D-I-X-I-E . . .

"How about this one?" I yelled out.

I'm just wild about Harry
and Harry's wild about me.

Harry was grinning from ear to ear. Suddenly I said, "Harry, you sound like you've done romancing. Did you ever think of getting married?"

"Sure, Steve — I coulda got married, but my mother wouldn't let me."

"When was that, Harry?"

"Aww, I was about twenty-five." He added, "I worked in a haberdashery, Steve."

"What kind of girl was she, Harry?"

"She was a nice girl, Steve."

"Why wouldn't your mother let you marry her?"

"She wasn't Jewish, Steve — and . . . and . . . she didn't think I should get married."

"Were you a religious family, Harry?"

"My father and mother were, Steve. My grandfather gave me a gold watch for my Bar Mitzvah . . . and . . . it was stolen."

"Your gold watch was stolen?"

"Yes, Steve."

"Did you ever get it back?"

"No, Steve."

Harry started to reminisce. It took him into other episodes. He remembered getting drunk at the age of thirteen. One evening his father and mother went to visit friends and left Harry at home by himself. Harry, as other boys do, went exploring through the house and came upon a bottle of sweet wine. He thought the bottle had soda in it and drank some of it. By the time his parents came home Harry was swinging on the chandelier.

"The next year," Harry explained, "I got sleeping sickness — and the year after I got polio."

"That must have been awful, Harry — you certainly got a bad break."

And that's the way it went until I got up to leave. It was Harry's cue to rise out of his chair and make the painful journey to his bed. Suddenly he blurted out, "You're my God, Steve, you're my God," and tried to kiss my hand.

"Don't do that, Harry," I said, horrified.

"You're my God, Steve," he repeated, his large, slightly bulging blue eyes staring at me.

"Cut it out, Harry, will you? Listen," I said, "don't be so grateful to me. I'm just a bum like anybody else, d'you see?"

Harry's eyes looked a little misty.

I went on. "Listen, there's only one God, and he made you and me. He made us alike at the same time that he made us different, although he put us in life situations so different from one another that sometimes I wonder whether we all belong to the same human race. But we do, Harry."

Harry seemed to be on the verge of tears.

"Harry, look," I said, "let's say a prayer to the Lord God together. Okay?"

8

I walked in Harry's apartment one Thursday evening, expecting to surprise him with a jumbo bottle of Coca-Cola. He wasn't there. A note addressed to me lay on the kitchen table. It read:

> Steve,
>
> Please call me if you have the chance.
>
> Sylvia, Harry's sister

I went down to the corner drugstore and called. A woman with a pleasant voice answered and identified herself as Sylvia. She got right to the point: Harry had had a slight stroke — his third in less than five years — and was resting comfortably at Jacobi Hospital.

"When can I visit him?" I asked.

"Any time," came the reply.

Saturday arrived, and I found myself walking down long hospital corridors, looking for Harry. The air reeked of antiseptics and detergents, giving the hospital an unnatural, chemical atmosphere. Hospitals are not pleasant places to visit. They are places where suffering wears no disguise; the blood and pus and bandages are in full view.

Harry was in Ward 406. He lay on his back, slightly raised, peeping out at the world from his bed. His defective right hand was tucked like a napkin over his chest. He didn't see me until I was right next to him.

When he saw me, his face brightened. He raised his head from the pillow, and shouted, "Hi Steve, hi Steve, hi Steve!"

I grabbed his hand and pumped it. "Harry, how are you?"

His face twisted with anguish, as it always did, as if he were about to impart an earthshaking message. Instead, he said, "Fine, Steve." Then he put his head back on the pillow, never taking his eyes from me.

I tried to understand why he kept his eyes on me so intensely. Perhaps he feared that if he took his eyes from me he would miss something, as though I were in some way his conduit to reality.

I said, "It's good to see you, Harry."

I'd been there a few minutes when Harry's sister Sylvia and her husband Jack entered the ward.

"I'm so glad to meet you," Sylvia said, stepping toward me.

Jack pointed to me and said, "This is Steve, Harry's friend."

Sylvia looked me over. "So you're Harry's friend." She turned to Harry and said, "Hello, Harry, how are you?"

Harry didn't answer. He was glaring at Jack. Suddenly he lifted his head from the pillow and spit these words out, "Ya not gonna railroad me. I'll never go; you'll never make me." His voice had risen to a shout. Patients and visitors turned in our direction.

Sylvia turned to me. "Oh, he doesn't want to go to a nursing home. That's his fear." She added dryly, "He doesn't have to worry."

Jack, who was getting the brunt of Harry's attack, said, "Oh shut up, ya bum. You ain't goin' nowhere."

At this, Harry aimed another volley of scurrilous words at Jack. He seemed to have been waiting for the chance to give Jack a piece of his mind, because he had all his words ready.

"All Jack said . . . " Sylvia started to say. Turning to me, Sylvia felt she had to explain. "All Jack said was, how would Harry like to go to the Poconos for a few weeks of vacation? But he thinks we're trying to get rid of him."

"Ya are," Harry snarled. "Ya *are* tryin' to get rid of me." But his eyes were on Jack, who had turned his back and was looking the other way.

Harry demonstrated something that afternoon: he had a temper.

Visiting him at the hospital the following week, I brought Harry a box of cherries. He ate one cherry, and said, "Give the rest to the others."

I said, "Okay," and went around to each patient with the box of cherries, saying "Take one."

I came to a young boy about eleven or twelve years old. The boy had huge, luminously brown eyes in a thin, white face. There was something very odd about the boy. He sat straight up in bed with his eyes staring straight ahead; he seemed to be gazing into his own private vision. The look on his face, of inward seeing, was so strange that I almost passed by him. I peered into his staring eyes and offered him a cherry, and watched him come out of himself like a person abruptly awakened. Suddenly he was smiling and thanking me, even before he saw the proffered cherry. He took one, and I went to the next patient. I turned to see whether the boy had put the cherry into his mouth. He hadn't. The boy was staring deeply into his vision.

The following Saturday when I came to visit Harry I saw that the boy's bed was now occupied by a different patient. I asked Harry what had happened to the boy.

"He died, Steve," Harry said, with that grimace and anguish of energy which it took him to say even the simplest things.

I was shocked. I asked one of the nurses what the boy had died of.

"He died of leukemia," she said. It gave me quite a turn.

I went back to Harry's bedside and asked, "How are they treating you, Harry?" But I didn't really listen to his reply. My thoughts were on the boy. I was trying to understand his death, but I couldn't make head or tale of it. How odd that the boy's life should be taken away when it had scarcely begun. Why is one given life if one can't finish that life? What meaning is there to a life that does not complete itself? I looked at poor Harry, his twisted, withered body poured out like a sack of potatoes onto that narrow hospital bed, and shook my head. This fellow too, I thought, has never had a chance. Never! What could Harry have done that his life should come to this? Even convicts serve their time and are given paroles. What is Harry given? Why, more time. He once said he had spent the best years of his life in a hospital. Is it any wonder he hated hospitals?

My face must have reflected my disturbing thoughts because Harry, who had been watching me the whole time, smiled. I smiled back, and right there I left the troubling problem of Harry's and the boy's unfair destinies unanswered.

9

Harry spent three months at Jacobi Hospital. He seemed to have complications, the nature of which was made a mystery by his doctors. Harry was shuttled from one ward to another. In fact, no one knew where he'd be at the next visit. His sister and her husband wanted him to remain in the hospital, believing he would get better care there. Harry, on the other hand, languished in his desire to return home. Every time I saw him he would repeat his lament: "I want to go home, Steve."

When I thought of his apartment, slightly more adorned than a prison cell, I found it hard to believe that Harry yearned to be there. Yet, staying in a hospital was no fun. How his days were spent in the stifling heat of summer I can only guess. I spent only one or two hours a week visiting with him in that antiseptic atmosphere, and that was oppressive enough for me. I wondered what it must have been like having to spend three months there. At the end of a visit with Harry I could shake his hand and leave him, grateful to return to my own circumstances.

At last came the long-awaited day for Harry's discharge from the hospital. The next time I came to see him he was home, enthroned once more in his easy chair, and beaming happily.

"Hi Steve, hi Steve!" he said. Harry was jubilant: he had come home. As for the nursing home — the one thing he dreaded more than anything — it hadn't come to pass.

For some weeks Harry didn't go to his corner on 86th Street and Lexington Avenue. I tried to discourage him from returning there.

"You don't have to go, do you, Harry?" I said. "Why don't you rest for a few months? Then you can go to work."

"Yes sir, champ," Harry said. But the following week he joyfully informed me that he had spent four hours "working."

Suddenly his mood changed. "I'm tired, Steve," he said glumly.

I seized the chance. "You should be, Harry — you just got out of a hospital. You should take a long rest before you go out again."

Harry agreed with me that he should rest. But the following week when I saw him, he bragged that he had been at work three different mornings. I found this baffling. But when I thought about it I began to understand Harry's need to work, no matter how much it tired him. To Harry, it meant life; it meant seeing people; it meant not having to be by himself day in and day out. Surely it could not have been the money that made him stand for four hours on one leg. (The "money" was ludicrously little. He averaged three to six dollars in a morning. On holidays, especially Christmas, he made more.) Those four hours, however, meant escape from the silence and bleakness of his two rooms, from noises floating up from the streets that must have seemed to him a faraway world of which he could have no part, from neighbors he couldn't join, from friends he couldn't have made even if he had tried. Indeed, even if he could have joined the people who lived around him, what did he have in common with them to talk about? Not to mention Harry's speech, which, even after two years of weekly visits, I still had trouble understanding.

On the corner of 86th and Lexington, however, there was always a chance that something would happen to Harry, something nice. He didn't have to do anything but stand there: life either came to him — or it didn't. Even if nothing special happened, it didn't matter because the world in a way revolved around him, and he would take it all in as best he could. He picked up words and fragments of conversation as people passed by or stood at the subway entrance. He heard tooting horns and screeching autos, felt the changing weather. And once in a while someone would stop and talk to him, perhaps seeing him as something more than a nondescript panhandler.

On this particular evening Harry became excited when I asked him if he had met any famous people during the course of his work. His eyes saw ahead of the words struggling to come out and be heard.

"Yes sir, champ," he finally said. "Yes sir." His body

worked and strained in his chair as he worked to claim my absolute attention.

"Tell me, Harry, who were they?"

"I knew them all, Steve." Harry tried to make you feel something of his accomplishment. His whole manner suggested that all the people worth knowing had been to Harry's street corner.

"Why, I knew Robert F. Kennedy."

"Did you now, Harry? What sort of fellow was he?"

Here he revealed a knack for putting together words for rhetorical effect:

"He was a swell man,
he was a great man,
he was a good man."

"Did he stop to talk to you?"

"No sir."

"He didn't talk to you?"

"No sir."

"Then what did he do?"

"He shook my hand," Harry said proudly.

"Who else did you meet, Harry?"

"Why . . . uh . . . uh . . . uh . . . " he floundered, then exploded: "Rockefeller!"

"You mean Nelson Rockefeller?"

"No, John D. Rockefeller, his father."

"Where did you meet these famous people, Harry? At 86th?"

"No, Steve."

After several minutes I was able to make out the words, "47th Street and Broadway." That was his old working corner.

"Rockefeller," I repeated the name. "Gee, Harry, that must have been a long time ago."

"Yup."

"Who else did you meet, Harry?"

Harry searched, " . . . uh . . . uh." His face brightened as he thought of a name: "Buddy Hackett. He was nice to me and . . . uh . . . uh," he rolled his blue eyes as another name came to mind, "Alan King."

He watched me to see the effect these famous names were having on me. He went on. "And George Jessel," he blurted out. Again his face brightened at the recollection. "He called me 'Slugger.' "

"Who?"

"Georgie Jessel." Another name exploded on his lips: "Eddie Cantor!" He added, "I knew him well."

I couldn't help asking him, "Did these fellows all give you money?"

"Yup!"

He suddenly shouted out another name. "Al Jolson! Al Jolson! I knew him, too." Harry looked happy just thinking about it.

"How long ago was that?"

"What?"

"How long ago did you know Al Jolson?"

Harry thought about it before he answered: "It was . . . uh . . . uh . . . " but I couldn't make out what he said. Harry repeated it, but all I could get from him was a jumble of words.

I tried to change the subject, but Harry wasn't easy to stop once he had made up his mind on anything. He kept saying it over and over until the words leaped at me in bold, clear relief. He had seen Al Jolson and spoken with him briefly in the street some fifteen years earlier, in 1952. Harry's eyes glowed; he was completely happy. Nothing gave him greater satisfaction than when he could convey information to another human being.

I couldn't help asking him another question, for I pictured those years in which this solitary, helpless man was left more or less at the mercy of scores of strangers, many of whom could not care less whether Harry could walk or talk, ate or starved, lived or died.

"In all that time, Harry," I asked, "what have you learned about people?"

I remember his answer word for word, especially because he said it without a trace of bitterness or irony.

"They were all kind toward me," he said. "Yup."

10

One morning I woke up to a mystery. Every morning upon waking, I first make coffee, then wash, dress, and last of all put on my shoes. Then I put on my coat and go to work. This morning, however, I noticed something different about my shoes: they were neatly placed in the corner under the living-room chair where I had taken them off the night before. But — and this is what I found peculiar — the lace of one shoe was neatly tied, while the other one was untied. I picked up the shoe with the tied lace and looked at it. How could I have taken the shoe off my foot with the shoelace tightly fastened? True, I might have done it unconsciously, for I had been tired the night before. Still, how could I have reversed a habit of years in this one particular detail? If I had taken the trouble to unlace one shoe in order to remove it from my foot, why hadn't I done the same with the other shoe?

To test out my assumption, I tried to put on the laced shoe. It wouldn't go on. Then I proceeded to unlace the shoe, put it on, lace it, and try to take it off. I had to pull and tussle with the shoe before I finally managed to yank it off. How could I have done this the night before and not remember it?

I looked at the shoes, first the one, then the other, and shrugged. I thought to myself, there must be a reasonable explanation for this even if I don't see it. Perhaps I am making more of this than I need to. So I put on my shoes and coat, and went to work.

When I went to see Harry that evening I found him unusually quiet. He greeted me warmly, but some of his explosive enthusiasm was lacking. He said, "Hi Steve, hi champ," but then he lowered his eyes and fell silent. I could see that there was something bothering him, so I thought I would leave him alone. If he had anything he wanted to tell me, he'd come out with it. I tore open his TV-dinner package of spaghetti and fish cakes, and made light talk about the weather, the rush hour, harassments of the day, etc.

A while later, as I was taking his dinner out of the oven, Harry said, "My brother died, Steve."

He sat back in the chair with his slightly bulging blue eyes staring intently at me. He then tried to explain what had happened to him in the past few days. His story, as I gathered it bit by bit, wasn't very nice.

To begin with, the weather the previous week had been unusually cold. On Saturday the temperature had dived to zero. Then it went up and the snow fell. It snowed all night, into Sunday. By Monday morning the city was snowbound, streets and highways impassable. Neither Sylvia nor Jack was able to reach their business which was located near Harry's apartment building; they were snowbound at their home in Mount Vernon. This left Harry in virtual isolation. He had no telephone, and had run out of food over the weekend, so all day Monday he starved. I doubt that he was even able to get up to make himself a cup of tea.

The next day, Tuesday, his sister Sylvia came with food. She also brought him the news about their brother, Morris. Morris had died early Monday morning at the height of the snowstorm.

Harry broke off his strenuous efforts to tell me what had happened, then picked it up again. His brother Morris, Harry explained to me, had been living with another sister in Florida when he died. Harry again hesitated, mumbled something, then fell silent.

"I'm sorry to hear about your brother, Harry," I said. "What caused his death?"

"A heart attack."

"What sort of work did he do?"

"He was in the shoe business, Steve. . . . " Suddenly Harry blurted out, "I can't lie to you, Steve, I can't lie to you."

I stared at him. I couldn't imagine what he was talking about.

"Steve," Harry said, "my brother died in Creedmore. I was ashamed to tell you."

"For Pete's sake, Harry, there's no shame in that. I had an uncle who died in Creedmore — poor fellow."

"Yeah?"

"Sure. I'll tell you about it sometime."

Harry then proceeded to tell me as best he could what had really happened to his brother. For many years Morris drove a taxicab for a living. Twelve years before he died he was in an auto accident and cracked his skull. He began acting strangely, and his family soon found it difficult to control him. He was sent to Creedmore.

"I was ashamed to say, Steve," Harry kept repeating over and over again. He exploded with the words, "My brother once did sell shoes, Steve. My sister owned the store. . . ."

Harry fell silent. He turned and pretended to watch television. I took his TV dinner out of the oven and placed it on the table, and lowered the volume on the television. We said the Lord's Prayer, and Harry said the words a little ahead of me to show that he knew the prayer by heart. This always touched me. After the Lord's Prayer we prayed that his brother, Morris, who had suffered so much in life, was at peace with God.

Harry ate his dinner in silence. I didn't want to bother him about his brother. I knew that Harry could get very self-conscious about the way he ate, so I talked to him about other, trivial things.

But as I sat watching him eat, I could not help thinking, *How sad that even when he eats, he is not entirely free from frustration.* Apart from his bad teeth, which hampered him in his chewing, he also had his lack of coordination to worry about. Even with his good hand, he had trouble picking up the food. His fork would sometimes miss the scrap. When he managed to get the scrap speared securely on his fork he would carry it to his mouth slowly, tortuously. Alas, it didn't always reach his mouth. Harry would assume that his mouth was open to receive the scrap of food. But what often happened is that his mouth didn't always coordinate with his hand. Sometimes the scrap reached a mouth that was pursed closed, although Harry didn't know it. When that happened, the piece of food would bang against his closed mouth and fall off the fork onto his shirt. Then the same painful process would start all over again. Fortunately, this did not happen most of the time.

When he finished his dinner, I raised the volume on the television and we watched the program that was on. After a while I got up and said that I had to go home.

"Why don't you stay, Steve?" Harry pleaded.

Sometimes I did stay a while longer, usually until about 7:30. During the week Harry's brother-in-law arrived at about six and put Harry to bed. When I came on Thursdays it was up to me to see Harry to bed. This meant standing next to him on his way to the bed to make sure he didn't fall. That's all there was to it. My getting ready to leave signaled that it was time for Harry to make the trip over to the bed. He didn't have to, of course. But since he had fallen on his way to bed other times, he didn't like to risk doing it alone.

With me standing by, Harry struggled out of his easy chair with the help of his crutch. Once he was on his good foot, he balanced himself with the crutch and turned himself slowly around. I turned off the television. Step by step Harry made his way to the bed, dragging his trembling, withered right leg. When he reached the bed he threw himself onto it. Then, twisting and turning with great difficulty, he rolled over and got under the covers. Once he was safe in bed I grabbed his hand and squeezed it. Sometimes I bent down and kissed him on the forehead. Harry said, "God love you, Steve," and I said, "And God love you, Harry. Sleep well."

11

That same night — it had been a long, wearying day — I picked up a book and read until midnight. Then I went to sleep.

About three o'clock in the morning I woke up and went to the bathroom. When I got back into bed and under the covers, my head no sooner touched the pillow when I heard a sound like *tap-tap, tap-tap*. It so startled me that I raised my head from the pillow to hear better. Sure enough, it was a clear, sharp sound, *tap-tap, tap-tap*. Someone was tapping on the window.

Good Lord, I thought to myself, what in heaven's name for! Why take the trouble to climb a fifth-floor fire escape when it would be easier to come to the door?

My bed was to the right of the window, so I had to get out of bed to see who was there. I looked out, but in the dim light I could see no one. It occurred to me that a dog or cat might have struck the windowpane with its paw. But I dismissed that possibility; the sounds had been so distinct and deliberate. The tapping sound had stopped from the moment I got out of bed.

I slipped back into bed, pulled the covers over me, and closed my eyes. Well, I thought to myself, when I rose from a sound sleep to visit the bathroom maybe I had still been half-dreaming. If so, then the tapping I heard so distinctly might have come from the borderline of my unconscious. I turned over on my side, took a deep breath, and decided I would go back to sleep.

But the instant I turned over, the tapping started again, sharp and insistent. Again I got out of bed and looked out the window. No one. It was right then, as I got back into bed, that I had the extraordinary perception that the spirit of Morris, Harry's brother who had died several days ago, was in the room with me. The thought really terrified me. I slid back into bed, shivering. At once I felt a strange movement of air pass over my face. The window, however, was closed from top to bottom. I lay in bed, numb with fear. Yet, the moment Morris entered my mind, I made the decision to have a Catholic Mass for the dead said for him — and that is when the tapping ceased. Nor did it start up again. I lay awake and prayed. Then I fell asleep.

12

In the morning I woke, clearly remembering what had happened during the night. I got out of bed and went to the window. I tapped it with my finger: *tap-tap, tap-tap*. The sound it made was the same as the one I had heard at three o'clock in the morning. The room was bare except for the bed and chest of drawers, and so there was a slight echo that had the same texture of sound I had heard during the night.

I stood there and gazed out the window at the beautiful morning. Morning is a wonderful witness to the known and familiar. But what in heaven's name had happened the night before? Had Harry's brother Morris come to me? Had he telepathically communicated with me, or had I literally dreamed it up? Had I discerned the spirit of Morris Guttenplan in my bedroom, and had it truly been Morris tapping on my window to win my attention?

Well, I *had* heard tapping sounds at my bedroom window. And I *had* immediately connected the tapping with Morris and with having a Mass said for him. As a Christian, I gave the incident an interpretation that is in keeping with the Gospels and Church teaching.

The Roman Catholic Mass is a prayer of sacrifice; it underscores the mystery of the Cross, the sacrifice Christ made for love of all humankind, and is our celebration and remembrance of this sacrifice. As well as being our bodily and spiritual connection in this life with Christ's suffering even unto death, the Mass brings us to the fulfillment of the Cross: resurrection unto life everlasting!

It is my belief that Christ reaches out to all people, particularly in their suffering and death, no matter what their religion happens to be, and that he uses those of us whom he can as instruments of his love. Something, then, on the other side of death must have informed Morris of what he had to do. He must have had some assurance that once I knew what it was he wanted, I would comply.

Standing there looking out the window, I suddenly remembered Harry saying that his brother Morris had sold shoes for a living. I went to have a look at my shoes. I didn't expect to see them tightly laced, and I was right; they weren't.

On my way to work that morning, I stopped at Saint Stephen's Church to have a Mass said for Morris. In the rectory I couldn't help telling the priest what had happened the night before. I asked him what he thought about it, adding, ''I hope I'm not going crazy.''

The priest, a white-haired, bespeckled man with a red

face, stared at me. "Well," he said slowly, "crazy or not, it won't harm to have a Mass said for this man."

On the Mass card he wrote the name of the deceased and the name of the priest who was to say the Mass, and handed the card to me. The inscription on the inside of the card read:

The Holy Sacrifice of the Mass will be offered for the repose of the soul of Morris Guttenplan.

I gave the priest the one-dollar fee, thanked him, and hurried out.

13

When I walked into Harry's apartment the following Thursday evening, the first thing he said was: "Guess what, Steve?"

"What?"

He said, "I dreamt of my brother Morris."

I had put a hamburger dinner in the oven. Now I came over near Harry and sat down.

"What did you dream about, Harry?"

"I dreamt of my brother . . . uh . . . uh . . . ." His voice trailed off. Then suddenly the words exploded on his lips: "He said he was gonna go to heaven soon."

I looked at Harry, searching his face to see whether he was kidding me. Harry looked at me wide-eyed, without a trace of humor or irony in his face.

"What else did he say?"

"That's all, Steve."

"He didn't say anything else?"

"No, Steve." Harry hadn't changed his expression of wide-eyed innocence.

"Well, that's great, Harry," I said, getting up to take his dinner out of the oven. "We all hope to go to heaven someday."

I left Harry's that evening very moved. I was especially taken by the dream he had had of his brother. How does one explain it? Could Harry have known anything about the Catholic doctrine of purgatory?

I doubt it. Harry was a poor, sick man who couldn't have been informed on such matters. He was also a Jew. In Jewish theology heaven is a possibility, not a certainty. On the whole, Jewish people are suspicious of religions which place more emphasis on the reality of heaven than on dealing with the realities of life. Harry had no doubt heard of heaven. Even the most primitive of peoples envision some kind of heaven, and primitive religions lay down conditions that must be fulfilled in order to obtain the gift of heavenly life.

In that light, it would have been no surprise if Harry's dream had fulfilled his wish-fantasy — if, in the dream, Morris had announced what Harry wanted to hear: that Morris was in heaven. But the dream did no such thing. Instead, it said that Morris would be going to heaven "soon," suggesting that some kind of time interval would elapse before he arrived there.

For nearly 2,000 years the Church has maintained that after death a soul undergoes a process of purification which prepares it for heaven. But Harry almost certainly knew nothing about this Catholic belief. So, it is indeed interesting that his dream presented Morris as acceptable for heaven but not yet ready for it.

All of this convinces me that Harry's dream about Morris was no fluke of his unconscious, but a real message from his brother who was in the transtemporal state, an interim period in which the dead discover the course they are to take in their afterlife journey. The message wasn't intended only for Harry, who was to die a little more than a year later; it was also meant for me.

I had been struggling for years to understand the mystery of death. Faith in Christ and in life everlasting is a gift, true. Nevertheless, the utter finality of bodily death is hard to reconcile with notions of afterlife. The curious situation in which I found myself — caught between two brothers passing messages to each other across the barrier of death — brought me face-to-face with the spiritual implications of these occurrences. This drama between the two brothers had one more scene, one final act, and it was to take place with Harry's death.

14

"I tell you, life is an awful thing," I said. Harry sat in his armchair, watching me pace the floor. Complaining from time to time was a habit of mine. I complained to God; I complained to myself; I complained to anybody who would hear me. "Yes, Harry — it stinks, the whole bit, it stinks — damn it!"

Actually, these were covert accusations aimed at God. Why did he create us? What was in it for him? Why allow such suffering in the world — especially of the innocent and helpless? And what of the victims of poverty, cruelty, stupidity, war? Why does God leave the innocent and helpless of this world at the mercy of an evil world? And so forth.

I ranted and paced the floor. I had reached a certain comfortable familiarity with Harry. I felt he wouldn't mind if I bellowed a little.

Harry sat watching me pace back and forth muttering under my breath the whole time. Suddenly he leaned back in his chair and said, "Look at me, Steve — I can't even move." I stopped my pacing and looked. Harry was right: he couldn't even move. He was able to move only his left hand, but the rest of him — bone, cartilage, tendon, nerve — was tacked together piece by piece. He was totally immobilized. Just going to the bathroom was a complicated operation.

Harry appeared to be genuinely surprised to hear me complaining. For him it was simple logic: sure, life is lousy, full of injustice and cruelty; but at least I could move myself across the floor. I could go here and there, with nothing to stop me. I was able to shout out my criticisms and accusations and have no difficulty being understood by God or man. Harry, in contrast, couldn't even get out of his chair or speak without enormous difficulty.

The next time I came to visit him, I found Harry in a quiet, thoughtful mood.

"What are you thinking about, Harry?" I asked. "You look down today."

Harry didn't answer right away. He stared at the window — mumbled something under his breath. I thought he was going to have another seizure. Instead he blurted out, "I feel so alone, Steve." Then in a low and subdued voice he said, "Steve, I'm gonna die." His words shook me.

His intuition was correct. Harry had only a year more to live, and it was once again his luck that he was to spend it in a hospital. He had started his life in a hospital, and he was to end it there. How explain such a man's life?

Harry was dragged back to the hospital like a convict to serve more time. What had he done? Nothing. He had simply been born with a very defective body, and this defective body denied him that portion of life that most people take for granted.

In even the most wretched of lives there is a high point, a moment in which people can say that they are happy to be alive, that they have experienced something so good that it is all worth the trouble. But in Harry's life — and no doubt this is a presumption on my part — there seemed to be no situation to mitigate it, to relieve it, no pause in his succession of bad luck. He brought his handicaps with him when he left the hospital as a child, but he didn't triumph over them as some other people apparently do. On the contrary, his life situation worsened, his handicaps multiplied. He went right on deteriorating until the very end of his life.

One April day Harry's sister, Sylvia, walked in to find him slumped on the floor, unconscious. He was taken to a hospital in the South Bronx. Doctors worked to save him from the effects of dehydration. Harry nearly died.

He spent the next seven months in that hospital, probably the most miserable time of his entire life. The hospital was overcrowded, had few doctors, inefficient nurses, and aides that only occasionally cleaned things up. Once I saw a rat as big as a groundhog playing around just outside the hospital entrance.

The day Harry entered the hospital marked the final phase of his life. It had been a life of incredible suffering, but Harry seemed to endure it so matter-of-factly that one would think Harry hadn't noticed any of it. He had, of course. From the day he entered the hospital, Harry's decline was inexorable. Even his physical appearance changed.

But in his manner he was still the old Harry. "Hi Steve, hi champ!" the words exploded on his lips. His large, generous greeting promised so much. But he fizzled out by the time he got off his chest the one or two things he had been saving to tell me. He was like a man with a giant capacity for love who pumped himself up to give you some of it, but then was prevented by the clogged arteries and crooked, withered muscles of his body. All he could do was fix his great blue eyes on you. With his eyes he tried to say what was in his heart. His eyes sometimes seemed to say, "Here I am. I want to say so much and do so much, but I can't, I can't — and oh, how I wish I could!"

As for me, I had all my stock phrases on the tip of my tongue and used them faithfully every time I visited Harry. I couldn't pass beyond them. All I would say were things like, "How are you, Harry? How do you feel? Are they taking good care of you? What did you do today?"

Harry was always amused when I asked him, "What did you do today?" He would answer, "I'm all right, Steve," though a mischievous smile would play on the corners of his mouth. If I persisted and asked what he had done during the day, his smile faded and his mouth worked to pronounce the words that finally came out: "I didn't do nothin'." It was silly, of course, to ask him what he had done when it was clear that he had lain in bed all day. But I couldn't think of anything else to ask him.

* * * *

One day as I sat working at my desk I thought of Harry and began to weep. I had to get up and go into the file room because I didn't want anybody to see me. What I felt became clear to me later. I wept because a soul would soon be passing from the world, and the love I had for Harry was already feeling the hurt of his passing.

Weeks passed into months. Harry improved — at least that is what the doctors told him — because he spoke excitedly of going home. "They're gonna send me home soon, Steve, they're gonna send me home." But they didn't send him.

As time passed he became more and more depressed, and a strange silence sprang up between us. It was as if nothing I could say to him could change what was happening. I tried to cheer him up, but I couldn't. Harry lay in his bed like a stone. He barely acknowledged my presence when I came to visit him.

In vain I tried to think of something to say. Was there any good news I could give him? I had none that I thought would relate to him, nothing that I thought would interest him. Whatever suggested itself sounded tinny and false. Could I say he was going to get well? I could not. Even if the doctors discharged him and sent him home, what kind of life would he be returning to? It would mean returning to a dirty, dingy apartment that was not much bigger than a prison cell, where he spent most of the day and night entirely by himself. It would mean returning to a life in which his only activity would be to stand on a street corner on one leg for four hours.

I stood by his bed and brooded. Harry was chained to that bed for months on end, completely dependent on others to help him — told when to eat, when to sleep, when to go to the toilet. Was there no end to it?

One day, as I stood there thinking these things, Harry

turned his blue eyes on me. He said, "Hi champ, hi champ!" His eyes twinkled.

"H'ya doing, Harry?" I answered in the same light way. Harry had sensed these moods in me other times, and tried to divert them. He was often successful. How interesting that I who came to serve him was often the one who was served by him.

15

The hospital Harry was in became intolerable, what with the poor care he received there; and so, after six months of hassle and delay, Harry's sister Sylvia got him transferred to Beth Abraham Hospital. Beth Abraham was a paradise in contrast; it was a newer, certainly cleaner, and better-staffed hospital. Harry was no longer thrown into a ward as big as a dance hall with forty other patients, as at the other hospital. Now he shared a room with only one other patient.

He peeped up at me when I came into the room. "Hi Steve, hi Steve!" he yelled. He positively glowed with excitement. We shook hands.

"You look very good, Harry. They must be treating you well."

"They're treating me nice, Steve."

I tried to think of something else to say, but when you have said it all a hundred times before, you have the feeling of playacting a part. Our friendship had gotten to the point where I would share certain confidences with Harry, but even that was no help. At this point, what could I say about myself? I came from a world that he, to a considerable degree, had already departed.

"Have you had any visitors, Harry?"

"Yup, my sister and brother-in-law." The words came out clearly.

"That's good," I said. "Well, how do you like it here, Harry? Is it better than the other place?" Of course it was better. The other place was virtually a sewer hole.

"Sure."

"Are they taking better care of you?" They were, of course, bound to be taking better care of him.

"Yes, Steve."

And so it went.

I found out the following week that Harry had been moved to the Hirshman Building. When I came in, he greeted me as in times past. His being seemed to burst with enthusiasm; he went through all the gestures and movements of a man happy to see his visitor. And he had something to tell me. As always, he put all his energy into telling it, his face twisting into huge scowls and grimaces as the words exploded on his lips. When he got out what he wanted to say, his large, blue eyes twinkled with sly merriment. He knew that I sometimes found it hard to grasp his meaning and that I worried about it. "Ah," his eyes seemed to say, "let's see if you understand what I just said."

But as the weeks went by, Harry became quieter and more drawn into himself. He started to lose weight. His great squarish jaw started to sag and gnarl, and the flesh under his throat began to drop and hang loosely. As he shed pounds his big, good hand turned bony.

I went looking for the doctor to ask him why Harry was losing so much weight. The doctor's explanation was reasonable: Harry had been put on a diet in order to bring down his blood pressure. Nothing to worry about. Yes, but what about his general condition? Was he improving? And if he was, when would he be discharged? Harry was not ready to be discharged, the doctor replied, but he was holding his own well. "Don't worry," the doctor said, and he turned and walked down the corridor.

At that point I hadn't learned that Harry had Parkinson's Disease, which is why he had been transferred to the Hirshman Building. It just never occurred to me that Harry could have Parkinson's or any other disease on top of all the other things. When I did learn about it through one of the nurses, I immediately went looking for the doctor to find out whether the disease was a dangerous one.

Yes, the doctor said without looking at me, Harry had Parkinson's Disease. No, there was nothing to worry about, he was being treated with doses of L-Dopa.

Was he going to get better?

The doctor's hand waved me to go away. "Yes, yes," he said, "the disease is being treated."

16

I arrived to visit with Harry at mealtime. The truck containing the food trays stood against the wall in the corridor. Aides were passing the trays out — but not to Harry. He lay on his side facing the window, his eyes half-closed. The other patient lay turned the other way, asleep.

When Harry saw me, he raised his head and mumbled something. Then his head dropped back onto the pillow. His greeting was distracted, introspective, so different from his other greetings. It was as if many things were on his mind, demanding his attention, but because I had come to see him he would be polite.

I sat down by his bedside, looked at his half-closed eyes, and didn't know what to say. I hated to ask him the same questions, but it seemed awkward just to sit there and say nothing. So, in a low voice I put the usual questions to him: How are you? How are they treating you?

When I asked him whether he had had visitors, Harry's eyes opened wide. Then, as if to say "How could I have forgotten?" he said, "Oh — Morris." To make sure I heard him, he repeated it a little louder: *"Morris."* He remained with his head slightly raised from the pillow, gazing at me.

"Morris!" I almost shouted. "You mean your brother who last year . . . ?"

"Yes, Steve."

"How can you say that?" I almost called him crazy. Keeping my voice down, I said, "Are you sure, Harry? Are you sure you didn't dream it?"

Harry pointed with his left hand. "He was standing right where you are, Steve."

I looked at him closely, but he met my gaze directly. I said, "Did he say anything, Harry? Did he talk to you?"

"He said, 'Pray.' "

I looked into Harry's open face to see if there wasn't a trace of hysteria in it. But Harry, laying his head back, kept quietly looking into my eyes.

"Did he say anything else, Harry?"

"Nope."

"What did he say after he told you to pray?"

"He went away."

"You mean he disappeared?" I realized I was putting words in his mouth.

Harry repeated: "He went away."

"You mean he vanished? Just vanished?"

Harry kept silent. He looked at me, but didn't answer.

I don't know why I felt happy, but I did. I turned to Harry

and said, "Well, what you say is wonderful, Harry. See, your brother loves you, and God loves you, and your brother has given you good advice."

Harry seemed to have already forgotten about it. He was wide awake now, but peacefully at rest with his head thrown back on the pillow. What we had been in the habit of doing at his apartment just before Harry would eat his dinner, we now did together in this tiny hospital room: we prayed. In times past, it was I who would forget to pray and Harry who would remind me. Lately it was Harry who forgot.

"Do you want to say the Lord's Prayer with me, Harry?"

"Yes, Steve," he said.

"Our Father . . . ," I began.

Harry joined in, " . . . who art in heaven. . . ."

The patient in the next bed stirred, breathed heavily, and turned the other way, but he didn't waken.

"I pray you, heavenly Father," I said, "deliver us from our troubles. But if we must have these troubles, help us to bear them. Father, help us to hope and trust in you no matter how bad things seem. As you promised us that some day you would wipe away the tears in our eyes and we would know joy that no man can take from us, so now strengthen us. Heavenly Father, console us and give us heart and take away all fear in us. Amen."

"Amen," said Harry.

Harry then put his head back onto the pillow. I sat and watched him. About ten minutes passed. Harry's eyelids gently closed, opened unseeingly, then closed again.

"Harry? Harry?" I said in a low voice. "I have to go now. Do you hear? I have to go, I'll see you next week — okay?"

Harry put his hand out. I shook it.

"Good-bye now," I said.

Passing through the front entrance of the hospital, I walked in a daze the two blocks to the subway. Was it true that Harry had actually been visited by the apparition of his brother Morris who had been dead for over a year? Or had this merely been the hallucination of a very sick man? Harry didn't sound hallucinated or even slightly delirious. He sounded completely sober and self-contained. If, in fact, Harry had only imagined his brother appearing to him, the appearance was both timely and highly spiritual. Indeed, Morris had appeared to his dying brother at the right time and with the right advice, put in a single word: *Pray!*

If, let us suppose, Harry was having hallucinations or delusions, they certainly were not extravagant ones. Look at the sheer economy of the advice offered by Morris. Not a word wasted: *Pray.* Why should Morris, if Morris were only a delusion, advise such a thing when there were so many other more colorful and interesting things he could have advised?

The exhortation to pray was utterly without promises, utterly bare of image. Harry was, however, exhorted to pray for something. What? That he recover? It did not seem that Harry could hope to recover, or want to recover, at this point. Then what was it that Morris had exhorted Harry to pray for?

It seems to me that the exhortation came from a reality that has nothing to do with this world. Indeed, both the word and the appearance of Morris meant that another world had briefly confronted Harry. The advice to pray meant that that other world was opening to him.

17

I was shocked when I saw Harry the following week. His great mane of thick, bristly hair had been shorn. His bushy eyebrows had been shaved clean. His mustache was gone, too.

When I came into the room, Harry lay with his head folded in his chest like a Russian saint in an icon. He barely stirred when he saw me. His eyes, in fact, no longer bulged even a bit. With the loss in weight his slightly bloated face looked deflated, as though air had gone out of it, and his cheekbones had begun to show. His eyes were now the eyes of a child, luminous with innocence.

When I saw him wearing a low-cut hospital shirt and his head and face shorn of hair, I thought of pictures I had seen of

Jews looking out from behind barbed-wire fences in con-
centration camps: persons with shaved heads, dressed in
striped garb, thin as cadavers, staring out of large unfocused
eyes, their faces wearing an expression suggesting that the
human being in them had gone beyond mere suffering into
another world safely distant from the harsh, terrifying glare
of reality and was now waiting only for the body to die.
Harry looked exactly as I had seen those inmates in con-
centration camps look: decimated to skin and bone, with the
frailest of flesh covering him.

Harry died on a Sunday, April 29, 1970. He was sixty-
three years old. His sister, Sylvia, telephoned me the next
day. Would I care to attend the funeral? Yes, I said.

On Tuesday morning we sat in one of the rooms at the
funeral home, some thirty members of Harry's family,
waiting for the service to begin. Harry's body lay in a dark,
brown-colored coffin. Its lid was shut. A few people chatted
in low voices. All the men wore yarmulkes, Jewish skull-
caps, on their heads. I did, too.

Soon the rabbi came in, and the room quieted. He spoke in
a low voice. The homily was short. He spoke of the pain of
losing someone we love. I was surprised to hear my name
mentioned. I was described as Harry's faithful friend. I
struggled to keep back the tears. Poor Harry, I'd done so little
for him, had provided him the merest rudiments of human
friendship.

"May the fullness of peace from heaven with life be
granted to us and all Israel; and say ye, Amen." The rabbi

recited a few such lines from the Kaddish, the Jewish prayer for the dead. The funeral service was over.

At Mount Hebron Cemetery the rabbi again spoke a few words. We stood off a way from the site of Harry's grave. No one wept.

One of Harry's mourners, a nephew of his, explained to the assembled group the Jewish custom for burying the dead: the dead are buried without a tombstone for one year in order to give the soul of the departed a chance to find its place in the other world. At the end of the year a tombstone is placed on the grave, the assumption being that the soul is at peace; his memory can now be inscribed on stone. Appropriate prayers are then offered by the rabbi.

The year passed. Harry's family never called me to participate in his final resting-place rite. It wasn't necessary; my business had been with Harry. Besides, I knew that Harry had found his right place in the other world.

I don't any longer feel sorry for Harry — because I am sure that he is well. Harry is well. He has passed beyond the ways and places of this life. He is with the Mystery we call God.